SOUPS AND STARTERS

HAMLYN

COOK'S NOTES

OVEN TEMPERATURES

°C	°F	GAS MARK	
70 C	150 F	Low	–
80 C	175 F	Low	–
90 C	190 F	Low	–
100 C	200 F	¼	–
110 C	225 F	¼	Very slow
130 C	250 F	½	Very slow
150 C	275 F	1	Slow
160 C	300 F	2	Moderately slow
170 C	325 F	3	Moderately slow
180 C	350 F	4	Moderate
190 C	375 F	5	Moderately hot
200 C	400 F	6	Hot
220 C	425 F	7	Hot
230 C	450 F	8	Very hot
240 C	475 F	9	Very hot

MICROWAVE POWER SETTINGS

Power Level	Percentage	Numerical Setting
HIGH	100%	9
MEDIUM HIGH	75%	7
MEDIUM	50%	5
DEFROST	30%	3
LOW	10%	1

SOLID WEIGHT CONVERSIONS

METRIC	IMPERIAL
15 g	½ oz
25 g	1 oz
50 g	2 oz
100 g	4 oz/¼ lb
175 g	6 oz
225 g	8 oz/½ lb
350 g	12 oz
450 g	1 lb
575 g	1¼ lb
700 g	1½ lb
800 g	1¾ lb
900 g	2 lb

MICROWAVE

Microwave tips have been tested using a 650 watt microwave oven. Add 15 seconds per minute for 600 watt ovens and reduce the timings by 5-10 seconds per minute for 700 watt ovens.

LIQUID VOLUME CONVERSIONS

METRIC	IMPERIAL
25 ml	1 fl oz
50 ml	2 fl oz
125 ml	4 fl oz
150 ml	5 fl oz/¼ pt
175 ml	6 fl oz
225 ml	8 fl oz
300 ml	10 fl oz/½ pt
450 ml	15 fl oz/¾ pt
600 ml	20 fl oz/1pt
900 ml	1½ pt
1.2 l	2 pt
1.7 l	3 pt

AUSTRALIAN CUP CONVERSIONS

	METRIC	IMP
1 cup flour	150 g	5 oz
1 cup sugar, granulated	225 g	8 oz
1 cup sugar, caster	225 g	8 oz
1 cup sugar, icing	175 g	6 oz
1 cup sugar, soft brown	175 g	6 oz
1 cup butter	225 g	8 oz
1 cup honey, treacle	350 g	12 oz
1 cup fresh breadcrumbs	50 g	2 oz
1 cup uncooked rice	200 g	7 oz
1 cup dried fruit	175 g	6 oz
1 cup chopped nuts	100 g	4 oz
1 cup desiccated coconut	75 g	3 oz
1 cup liquid	250 ml	9 floz

WEIGHTS AND MEASURES

Metric and Imperial weights and measures are given throughout. Don't switch from one to the other within a recipe as they are not interchangeable. 1 tsp is the equivalent of a 5 ml spoon and 1 tbls equals a 15 ml spoon.

All spoon measurements are level, all flour plain, all sugar granulated and all eggs medium unless otherwise stated.

SYMBOLS

 FREEZER TIP

 SERVING SUGGESTION

 MICRO-WAVE TIP

 WINE & DRINK NOTE

CONTENTS

First published in Great Britain in 1993 by Hamlyn
an imprint of Reed Consumer Books Limited
Michelin House, 81 Fulham Road, London SW3 6RB
and Auckland, Melbourne, Singapore and Toronto

Reprinted 1993, 1994

Copyright © GE Fabbri Limited 1993
Photographs and text copyright © GE Fabbri Limited 1988, 1989, 1993

ISBN 0 600 57775 9

A CIP catalogue record for this book is available from the British Library

Produced by Mandarin Offset
Printed and bound in Singapore

TOMATO & BASIL SOUP

Martin Brigdale

This soup combines the sweetness of fresh basil with the tangy flavour of ripe tomatoes. Fromage blanc adds creaminess.

PREPARATION TIME: 15 MINS
COOKING TIME: 10 MINS
SERVES 6

I N G R E D I E N T S

2.3 KG/5 LB TOMATOES

24 LARGE BASIL LEAVES

175 G/6 OZ SALTED BUTTER

SALT AND GROUND BLACK PEPPER

75 G/3 OZ FROMAGE BLANC

into a frying-pan. Add 50 g/2 oz of the butter and place over a medium heat, shaking the pan and stirring.

3 When the tomato strips start to break up, turn up the heat and briskly stir in the rest of the butter. When all the butter has been added, the tomatoes should only be half cooked. Season with salt and pepper.

4 Fill individual soup bowls with the tomato soup, then spoon fromage blanc into the middle of each bowl. Garnish each soup bowl with a fresh basil leaf and serve at once.

1 Make a small slit in the skin of each tomato and blanch in boiling water for 5-7 seconds. They are ready when the skin starts to peel away from the knife slits. Lift the tomatoes out and peel, then halve, scooping the seeds and juice into a sieve set over a bowl. Sieve the juice and reserve, then cut the tomato flesh into small strips.

TIP

IF YOU WANT TO SKIN SMALLER QUANTITIES OF TOMATOES YOU WILL FIND IT QUICK AND EASY IF YOU CUT A CROSS ON THE TOPS OF THE TOMATOES, PUSH A FORK INTO THE OTHER END AND SEAR THE TOMATO SKIN OVER A MEDIUM GAS FLAME, TURNING THE TOMATO OVER AS THE SKIN LOOSENS.

 WARM SOME FRENCH BREAD IN THE OVEN, AND SERVE CHUNKS OF IT WITH THE SOUP.

m PUT TOMATO STRIPS, JUICE AND BASIL WITH 50 G/2 OZ OF THE BUTTER IN A LARGE MICROWAVE-PROOF BOWL, COVER AND COOK ON HIGH (100%) FOR 10 MINUTES. BEAT IN THE REST OF THE BUTTER AND COOK FOR A FURTHER 5-10 MINUTES UNTIL THE TOMATOES HAVE SOFTENED, SEASON AND SERVE WITH BREAD ROLLS WARMED IN THE MICROWAVE. SIX ROLLS WARMED ON DEFROST (30%) WILL TAKE 2-3 MINUTES. WARMING ON A LOW SETTING WILL PREVENT THE BREAD FROM DRYING OUT.

Paul Moon

2 Roughly chop all but 6 of the basil leaves. Put the tomato strips, reserved juice and chopped basil

FRESH PEA SOUP

James Murphy

A soup which capitalises on the wonderful flavour of fresh peas. It needs to be made just before serving and looks wonderful decorated with a swirl of cream.

PREPARATION TIME: 15 MINS
+ COOLING
COOKING TIME: 25 MINS
SERVES 6

INGREDIENTS

900 G/2 LB FRESH PEAS

50 G/2 OZ BUTTER

1 CLOVE OF GARLIC

1.4 L/2½ PT CHICKEN STOCK

150 ML/¼ PT DOUBLE CREAM, PLUS
EXTRA TO SERVE

SALT AND GROUND WHITE PEPPER

Peter Reilly

1 Shell the peas so you are left with about 450 g/1 lb. Put them in a saucepan with 175 ml/6 fl oz water and cook for 5 minutes until tender. Drain them over a jug keeping the liquid.

2 Melt the butter in a large saucepan. Add the garlic and peas and sauté gently over a low heat for 5 minutes. Add the chicken stock and water the peas boiled in. Bring to the boil, then reduce the heat and simmer the soup for 10 minutes.

3 Cool the soup then purée in a liquidiser or food processor, or push it through a sieve using a spoon. Return it to the pan with the cream, season and reheat it without boiling. To serve add a swirl of cream.

m PUT THE PEAS IN A BOWL AND POUR OVER 100 ML/4 FL OZ BOILING WATER. COVER AND MICROWAVE ON HIGH (100%) FOR 5-8 MINUTES UNTIL TENDER. STIR TWICE DURING COOKING. DRAIN AND KEEP THE LIQUID. MELT THE BUTTER IN A SHALLOW DISH FOR 45 SECONDS. ADD PEAS AND GARLIC, COVER AND COOK FOR 5 MINUTES. ADD BOILING STOCK AND RESERVED WATER, COVER AND MICROWAVE FOR 10 MINUTES, STIRRING TWICE DURING COOKING. LIQUIDISE THEN POUR INTO A BOWL, COVER AND REHEAT FOR 2 MINUTES, STIRRING ONCE. IF USING FROZEN PEAS, COOK WITHOUT DEFROSTING AND NO WATER, FOR 10 MINUTES.

TIP

IF USING FROZEN PEAS CHOOSE A 450 G/ 1 LB PACK AND DON'T BOTHER TO PRE-COOK THEM. JUST THAW AND SAUTE THE PEAS IN THE BUTTER. SERVE THE SOUP GARNISHED WITH CHERVIL INSTEAD OF THE SWIRL OF CREAM.

THICK CARROT & CORIANDER SOUP

Andrew Whittuck

This spicy soup can be made in less than an hour – ideal for the busy cook. Make twice as much as you need and freeze it down so that you always have a starter for unexpected guests.

PREPARATION TIME: 10 MINS
COOKING TIME: 30-40 MINS
SERVES 6

INGREDIENTS

50 G/2 OZ BUTTER
900 G/2 LB CARROTS, SLICED
1 LARGE ONION, CHOPPED
½ TSP CORIANDER POWDER
½ TSP CORIANDER SEEDS, CRUSHED
½ TSP GROUND GINGER
½ TSP GROUND MACE
1.4 L/2½ PT VEGETABLE STOCK
SALT AND GROUND BLACK PEPPER
150 ML/¼ PT SINGLE CREAM
FINELY CHOPPED CORIANDER LEAVES, TO GARNISH
CARROT, TO GARNISH

the stock and seasoning and simmer for 30-40 minutes or until the vegetables are very soft. Purée the soup in a liquidiser or food processor.

Diana Miller

 Reheat the soup until it is just boiling, then add the cream and sprinkle with the coriander leaves. Stamp pretty shapes out of the carrot with a small cutter, use to garnish then serve.

 Melt the butter in a saucepan, add the carrots and onion, cover with a lid and cook for 5 minutes.

Add the coriander powder and seeds, the ground ginger and mace and fry for 1 minute. Add

FREEZE THIS SOUP IN CONVENIENT INDIVIDUAL PORTIONS FOR UP TO 3 MONTHS. IT CAN THEN BE HEATED STRAIGHT FROM FROZEN.

PUT THE BUTTER, CARROTS AND ONION IN A MICROWAVE-PROOF BOWL AND COOK ON HIGH (100%) FOR 3 MINUTES. ADD THE SPICES AND COOK FOR 1 MORE MINUTE. BRING THE STOCK TO THE BOIL AND ADD TO THE BOWL THEN COOK FOR 12-14 MINUTES. COOL AND LIQUIDISE. TO REHEAT, COOK FOR 1 MINUTE THEN STIR IN THE CREAM.

CLASSIC ONION SOUP

Andrew Whittuck

Traditional onion soup is as economical as it is
simple. Poured over chunky slices of toasted
bread and cheese, it makes a warming
family snack or hearty first course when
friends come round to supper.

PREPARATION TIME: 10 MINS
COOKING TIME: 1 HOUR 20 MINS
SERVES 6

I N G R E D I E N T S

| 2 TBLS OIL |
| 25 G/1 OZ BUTTER |
| 700 G/1 LB 8 OZ ONIONS, SLICED |
| 2 TSP CASTER SUGAR |
| 2 CLOVES OF GARLIC, CRUSHED |
| 1.2 L/2 PT DARK VEGETABLE OR BEEF STOCK |
| 300 ML/½ PT DRY WHITE WINE |
| SALT AND GROUND BLACK PEPPER |
| 6 SLICES FRENCH BREAD |
| 225 G/8 OZ GRUYERE CHEESE, GRATED |

Peter Reilly

3 Five minutes before serving, set the grill to high. Cover the slices of bread with the cheese and grill until they are gold and bubbling.

4 To serve, lay a piece of the toasted bread in the bottom of each soup bowl and ladle the hot soup over it. Serve immediately, while the soup is piping hot.

m TO MAKE THE SOUP, PUT THE OIL, BUTTER, ONIONS AND SUGAR INTO A MICROWAVE-PROOF BOWL AND COOK ON HIGH (100%) FOR 3 MIN-UTES, STIRRING ONCE. ADD THE GARLIC AND COOK FOR 1 MINUTE. POUR IN THE STOCK AND WINE, SEASON, COVER AND COOK ON MEDIUM (50%) FOR 8 MINUTES.

WATCHPOINT

CARAMELISED ONIONS GIVE THE SOUP ITS GOLDEN COLOUR. IF YOU WANT A DEEPER BROWN, ADD THE ONION SKIN AND REMOVE JUST BEFORE SERVING.

1 Heat the oil and butter in a heavy-based saucepan. Add the onions and sugar and cook over a medium heat, stirring frequently, for 20 minutes or until they caramelise into an even brown colour. Add the garlic and fry for 1 more minute.

2 Add the stock, white wine and salt and pepper and simmer over a low heat for 1 hour.

TIP

THE CHEESE AND TOAST CAN BE GRILLED IN ADVANCE. THE BOILING SOUP WILL HEAT THE BREAD AND CHEESE.

CRAB CHOWDER

Clint Brown

Fresh crab meat helps to make soup into a
superb chowder. Use both the white and
brown meat or, to save time, buy prepared
crabmeat sold in the shell.

PREPARATION TIME: 10 MINS
COOKING TIME: 30 MINS
SERVES 6-8

INGREDIENTS

| 50 G/2 OZ SMOKED STREAKY BACON |
| 1 SMALL GREEN PEPPER |
| 350 G/12 OZ POTATOES |
| 25 G/1 OZ BUTTER |
| 1 ONION, FINELY CHOPPED |
| 1 TBLS FLOUR |
| 450 ML/¾ PT FISH STOCK |
| 450 ML/¾ PT HALF CREAM OR CREAMY MILK |
| SALT AND GROUND BLACK PEPPER |
| PINCH OF GRATED NUTMEG |
| PINCH OF CAYENNE PEPPER |
| 100 G/4 OZ CRAB MEAT |
| 300 G/11 OZ TINNED SWEETCORN, DRAINED |

2 Fry the bacon over a gentle heat in a large pan until the fat begins to run. Add the butter, and when melted, add the green pepper, potatoes and onion. Fry gently for 7-8 minutes until slightly softened, stirring occasionally.

3 Sprinkle the flour over the bacon and vegetables and then stir for a few minutes until the mixture becomes golden and frothy. Blend the fish stock with the cream and add to the pan with the seasoning and spices. Bring to the boil, cover and simmer for 15 minutes or until the vegetables are tender.

1 Trim the rind from the bacon and chop finely. Halve the green pepper, remove the seeds and cut into 6 mm/¼ in dice. Peel the potatoes and dice the same way.

4 Flake the crab meat and stir into the pan along with the tinned sweetcorn. Cook for a few minutes so it heats through, adjust the seasoning to taste and then serve.

SERVE THE CHOWDER WITH BROWN BREAD AND GARNISH WITH DILL. FOR A DINNER PARTY, SUBSTITUTE 150 ML/ ¼ PT OF THE FISH STOCK WITH DRY WHITE WINE.

LENTIL & BACON SOUP

Andrew Whittuck

Lentil & Bacon Soup – a substantial main meal soup – is nourishing and filling. Serve it to the family in winter to keep cold weather at bay.

PREPARATION TIME: 10 MINS
COOKING TIME: 40–50 MINS
SERVES 6

INGREDIENTS

225 G/8 OZ BROWN OR GREEN
LENTILS

150 ML/¼ PT OLIVE OIL

1 ONION, PEELED AND THINLY
SLICED

100 G/4 OZ THICK SLICE OF BACON,
DICED

2 CLOVES OF GARLIC, CHOPPED

2 CARROTS, PEELED AND SLICED
INTO 6 MM/¼ IN ROUNDS

1 CELERY STALK, SLICED INTO
6 MM/¼ IN PIECES

400 G/14 OZ TINNED TOMATOES

1 TBLS DRIED OREGANO

SALT AND GROUND BLACK PEPPER

FOR THE CROUTONS

2 THIN SLICES OF WHITE BREAD

OIL, FOR DEEP FRYING

2 In another large saucepan heat 2 tbls of the olive oil and cook the onion, bacon and half the garlic for 5 minutes. Add the remaining olive oil, garlic, carrots, celery, tomatoes, oregano, lentils, 1 L/1¾ pt water and seasoning. Cover and simmer for 30–40 minutes, until the lentils are soft.

Peter Reilly

3 Meanwhile make the croûtons. Heat the oil to 190 C/375 F. Remove the crusts from the bread and cut into 12 mm/½ in dice. Deep fry until the croûtons are an even light brown then remove the basket or use a slotted spoon and drain on kitchen paper. Sprinkle the croûtons over the soup before serving.

1 Put the lentils in a saucepan, cover with water and bring to the boil. Boil for 3 minutes then drain thoroughly.

TIP

FOR ADDED FLAVOUR, SHAKE THE CROU-
TONS IN SALT AND PEPPER AS THEY DRAIN
ON KITCHEN PAPER.

MINESTRONE

Michael Michaels

Serve minestrone soup with warm crusty bread, a crisp green salad and a glass of wine and it's a meal in itself.

**PREPARATION TIME: 20 MINS
+ SOAKING
COOKING TIME: 2½ HOURS
SERVES 4-6**

I N G R E D I E N T S

75 G/3 OZ DRIED WHITE HARICOT
BEANS, SOAKED OVERNIGHT

1 TBLS OLIVE OIL

1 ONION, FINELY SLICED

1 CLOVE OF GARLIC, CRUSHED

1 LARGE CARROT, FINELY DICED

1 STICK OF CELERY, FINELY DICED

1 COURGETTE, FINELY DICED

225 G/8 OZ TOMATOES, SKINNED AND
CHOPPED

2 TSP TOMATO PUREE

1.4 L/2½ PT VEGETABLE STOCK

50 G/2 OZ SHELLED PEAS

100 G/4 OZ POTATO, DICED

1-2 TBLS PASTA SHAPES

100 G/4 OZ CABBAGE, SHREDDED

1 TSP FRESHLY CHOPPED BASIL

1 TSP FRESHLY CHOPPED PARSLEY

SALT AND GROUND BLACK PEPPER

1 Drain the haricot beans, cover
with cold water and simmer for 1
hour until tender. Drain.

2 Heat the olive oil in a large
saucepan, add the onion and
garlic and cook over a low heat

for 5 minutes. Do now allow ingredients
to colour. Add the carrot, celery and
courgette and cook gently for 5 minutes.

3 Add the drained haricot beans,
tomatoes, tomato purée and stock
and bring to the boil. Simmer for
1 hour. Add the peas, diced potato and
pasta, and cook for 10 minutes. Add the
cabbage, basil and parsley. Season and
simmer for 5 minutes.

 FOR ADDED FLAVOUR,
SPRINKLE GRATED PARMESAN
CHEESE OVER THE SOUP JUST
BEFORE SERVING.

FRENCH FISH SOUP

Alan Newnham

Try this saffron-flavoured fish soup served
with Gruyère cheese and a garlicky rouille for
an authentic taste of the South of France.

PREPARATION TIME: 20 MINS
COOKING TIME: 25 MINS
SERVES 4-6

I N G R E D I E N T S

1.1 KG/2 LB 8 OZ MIXED FISH,
INCLUDING LANGOUSTINES,
MONKFISH, RED MULLET AND CRAB

2 TBLS OLIVE OIL

2 ONIONS, FINELY CHOPPED

2 CLOVES OF GARLIC, CRUSHED

2 SHALLOTS, FINELY CHOPPED

1 LEEK, FINELY SLICED

1 CELERY STALK, SLICED

1 CARROT, CHOPPED

2 TOMATOES, QUARTERED

5 CM/2 IN STRIP OF ORANGE PEEL

2 SPRIGS OF FENNEL

2 BAY LEAVES

PINCH OF SAFFRON STRANDS

SALT

CAYENNE PEPPER

1 Chop the mixed fish into 5 cm/2 in lengths. Crack the crab shell and break into small pieces.

2 Heat the oil in a large saucepan. Add the onions, garlic, shallots, leek, celery, carrot and tomatoes and fry gently for 5 minutes until soft.

3 Pour 1.2 L/2 pt water over the vegetables and bring to the boil. Add the fish, orange peel, fennel and bay leaves and boil for 15 minutes.

4 Using a slotted spoon, transfer all the fish (bones and all) and the crab meat and shell into a liquidiser. Grind them until the fish, crab and shell become a coarse pulp.

5 Stir the ground fish into the soup, then strain through a very fine sieve into a clean saucepan, pressing the fish with the back of a spoon to extract the liquid. Stir in the saffron and reheat gently. Season.

SERVE WITH TOASTED FRENCH BREAD COVERED WITH ROUILLE — A SAUCE MADE WITH GARLIC, OIL, CHILLIES, PIMIENTOS AND FRESH BREADCRUMBS — AND THEN TOPPED WITH MELTED GRUYERE CHEESE. FOR A QUICK AND EASY ROUILLE, COMBINE HOMEMADE MAYON-NAISE WITH CRUSHED GARLIC, PIMIENTO AND CAYENNE PEP-PER OR TABASCO.

PRAWN COCKTAIL ICE BOWL

Peter Reilly

Here's the ultimate version of everyone's favourite prawn cocktail. Serve it in this stylish and surprisingly easy-to-make ice bowl and impress and delight your dinner party guests.

PREPARATION TIME: 45 MINS +
FREEZING
SERVES 6

INGREDIENTS

FOR THE ICE BOWL
100 G/4 OZ UNPEELED PRAWNS
6 DILL FRONDS
1 SMALL LEMON, SLICED
FOR THE PRAWN COCKTAIL
2 TBLS DOUBLE CREAM
4 TBLS MAYONNAISE
1 TBLS TOMATO PUREE
CAYENNE PEPPER
2 TBLS LEMON JUICE
1 SMALL GALIA OR OGEN MELON
1 SMALL RED PEPPER, SLICED
1 RED APPLE, DICED
4 SMALL CELERY STALKS, SLICED
450 G/1 LB PRAWNS, THAWED IF FROZEN
6 LEAVES CURLY ENDIVE
PAPRIKA PEPPER
6 WHOLE PRAWNS, TO GARNISH

2 Meanwhile make the prawn cocktail: whip the cream and mix it with the mayonnaise, tomato purée, cayenne pepper and lemon juice.

Chris King

3 Using a melon baller, scoop the melon into balls. Mix them, together with the red pepper, apple, celery and prawns, with half the mayonnaise mixture.

Peter Reilly

1 Fill a 22 cm/8½ in bowl ⅓ full of very cold water. Put an 18 cm/7 in bowl inside the first and secure with tape. Push the unpeeled prawns and dill fronds in between the 2 bowls, make sure they are just covered in water and freeze. Add the lemon slices, top up with cold water and freeze again.

4 Unmould the ice bowl and line it with the curly endive leaves. Put the prawn cocktail mixture on top of the leaves, top with the rest of the mayonnaise mixture and sprinkle with paprika. Garnish with the whole prawns and serve immediately.

TIP

DON'T WORRY IF THE ICE BOWL CRACKS WHEN UNMOULDED. JUST RETURN IT TO THE FREEZER AND RE-FREEZE.

CHEAT'S POTTED PRAWNS

Alan Newnham

Fresh ginger makes this classic recipe different – and the cheat is that they don't need two days maturing before eating.

Peter Reilly

PREPARATION TIME: 15 MINS +
MARINATING
COOKING TIME: 8 MINS
SERVES 4

I N G R E D I E N T S

450 G/1 LB FROZEN PEELED PRAWNS
JUICE OF 1 LEMON
GROUND BLACK PEPPER
¼ NUTMEG, GRATED
2.5 CM/1 IN PIECE FRESH ROOT GINGER, PEELED AND GRATED
275 G/10 OZ BUTTER
12 FRESH CORIANDER LEAVES

1 Thaw the prawns and pat dry with kitchen paper to absorb excess water. Place them in a bowl with the lemon juice, black pepper, nutmeg and ginger, cover and leave to marinate in a cool place for ½ hour.

2 Drain off all the liquid. Melt 225 g/ 8 oz of the butter in a small frying-pan. Add the prawns and cook very gently for 5 minutes. Spoon the mixture into 4 ramekins. Chill until set.

3 Meanwhile, clarify the remaining butter. Line a small sieve with a doubled piece of muslin and set over a basin. Place the butter in a small pan over a gentle heat and when it is completely melted, pour it through the sieve. Discard the foamy white deposits.

4 When the potted prawns have almost set, brush the underside of the coriander leaves with a little clarified butter and garnish each ramekin with 3 leaves. Then carefully spoon clarified butter over the prawns so that it just coats them. Chill for another ½ hour and then serve.

TIP

POTTED PRAWNS FREEZE WELL FOR UP TO 3 MONTHS. THEY ALSO KEEP FOR 3-4 DAYS IN THE FRIDGE. NOT AT THEIR BEST COLD, MAKE SURE YOU BRING THE PRAWNS UP TO ROOM TEMPERATURE BEFORE EATING.

 FOR SIMPLE CANAPES, SPREAD ON BUTTERED TOAST AND GARNISH WITH GHERKIN OR PICKLED WALNUTS.

MUSHROOM & CHICKEN TERRINE

Paul Moon

This terrine, with mushrooms studded through it, has a firm texture which slices easily. Serve with lemon mayonnaise.

PREPARATION TIME: 35 MINS
COOKING TIME: 1-1½ HOURS
SERVES 6

INGREDIENTS

BUTTER, FOR GREASING
225 G/8 OZ BUTTON MUSHROOMS
275 G/10 OZ CHICKEN BREASTS
2 EGGS, BEATEN
SALT AND GROUND WHITE PEPPER
GRATED ZEST OF 1 ORANGE
60 ML/2½ FL OZ DOUBLE CREAM
25 G/1 OZ FRESH WHITE BREADCRUMBS
FOR THE LEMON MAYONNAISE
1 EGG YOLK
1 EGG
2 TBLS LEMON JUICE
½ TSP SALT
1 TSP DRY MUSTARD
GROUND WHITE PEPPER
300 ML/½ PT SUNFLOWER OIL

2 Place the loaf tin in a roasting tin. Butter 2 strips of greaseproof paper. Use 1 to line the loaf tin. Spoon the mixture into the loaf tin and cover with the other strip of greaseproof paper, buttered side down. Put water in the roasting tin to come halfway up the sides of the loaf tin. Cook for 1-1½ hours until firm.

3 Meanwhile make the lemon mayonnaise: blend together the egg yolk, egg, lemon juice, salt, mustard and white pepper at maximum speed for 5 seconds, or until mixed together well. With the blender still running, add the oil through the feeder tube of the machine, starting slowly with a fine steady trickle and then pour in a steady stream until all the oil has been added. This should take about 3 minutes.

1 Heat the oven to 170 C/325 F/Gas 3. Butter a 450 g/1 lb loaf tin. Halve the mushrooms. Finely mince the chicken breasts. Place in a large mixing bowl and stir in the eggs, seasoning, orange zest, double cream, breadcrumbs and mushrooms.

4 When the terrine is cooked, carefully unmould it and cut it into slices using a sharp knife. Serve it hot, or allow it to cool.

SERVE WITH TOSSED LEAF SALAD, ORANGE SLICES AND FLAT-LEAVED PARSLEY.

AVOCADO WITH TOMATO SAUCE

Alan Newnham

Nothing could be simpler than this elegant dish
– slices of avocado, fanned out over a
light tomato sauce.

PREPARATION TIME: 10 MINS
+ CHILLING
SERVES 4

INGREDIENTS

2 LARGE, RIPE, UNBLEMISHED
AVOCADOS

FOR THE SAUCE

400 G/14 OZ TINNED PLUM
TOMATOES

1 SHALLOT, CHOPPED

½ TSP SUGAR

1 TSP FRESH THYME

SALT AND GROUND BLACK PEPPER

1 First make the sauce: place the tomatoes and their juice, the shallot, sugar, thyme and salt and pepper in a food processor or blender and blend until smooth. Sieve, then chill in the fridge for 30 minutes.

2 Halve the avocados by slicing around the stone then twisting apart. Make a nest with a tea-towel on a chopping board and sit an avocado half in it. Hit the stone with a large cook's knife then ease it out.

3 Score the skin into segments with a small sharp knife then peel. The tougher the avocado skin, the narrower the strips need to be cut.

4 Place the peeled avocado halves on a plate and make equal lengthwise cuts, leaving the narrow end intact.

5 Gently push the avocado slices apart with your fingers so that the slices fan out. Surround with a pool of the sauce then serve.

TIP

TO PREVENT AVOCADOS DISCOLOURING
BRUSH WITH OIL OR LEMON JUICE.

THE TOMATO SAUCE CAN BE
SUCCESSFULLY FROZEN FOR
UP TO 6 MONTHS.

Diana Miller

PEARS WITH STILTON

Alan Newnham

Fresh mint, Stilton and juicy pears – a
trio of traditional ingredients used in an
unusual way.

PREPARATION TIME: 10 MINS
+ CHILLING
SERVES 4

INGREDIENTS

75 G/3 OZ STILTON CHEESE
75 G/3 OZ CREAM CHEESE
4 LARGE RIPE DESSERT PEARS
LEMON JUICE, FOR BRUSHING
4 FRESH MINT SPRIGS, TO GARNISH
FOR THE DRESSING
3 TBLS OIL
1 TBLS LEMON JUICE
1 TBLS CHOPPED FRESH MINT
1 TSP SUGAR
SALT AND GROUND BLACK PEPPER

lemon juice and then pipe in the soft cheese mixture. Chill in the fridge until ready to serve.

3 Meanwhile make the dressing: put the oil, lemon juice, chopped mint, sugar and salt and pepper in a screwtop jar. Shake vigorously, then adjust seasoning if necessary.

4 To serve, slice each pear across into thin round slices. Arrange on serving plates. Spoon the dressing over the top and garnish with sprigs of fresh mint.

 SERVE WITH A CHILLED DRY WHITE WINE, SUCH AS POUILLY FUME OR CHABLIS.

1 Beat together the Stilton and cream cheese until soft. Spoon into a piping bag fitted with a large plain nozzle.

2 Using an apple corer or melon baller scoop out the cores of the pears. Paint each hole with the

HORS D'OEUVRE PLATTER

Paul Moon

Traditionally, an hors d'oeuvre is served to whet the appetite before a main meal, and this colourful, refreshing platter certainly fits the bill.

PREPARATION TIME: 30 MINS
COOKING TIME: 6-8 MINS
SERVES 4-6

I N G R E D I E N T S

225 G/8 OZ GRATED CARROTS

6 TBLS OLIVE OIL

2 TBLS LEMON JUICE

2 TBLS FINELY CHOPPED FRESH
PARSLEY

1 LARGE CLOVE OF GARLIC, CRUSHED

SALT AND GROUND BLACK PEPPER

1 GREEN PEPPER

1 RED PEPPER

1 BEEFSTEAK TOMATO, CUT INTO
THIN WEDGES

1 TBLS CHOPPED FRESH BASIL

100 G/4 OZ MUSHROOMS, SKINNED

2 TBLS CAPERS

50 G/2 OZ BLACK OLIVES, STONED

400 G/14 OZ TINNED ARTICHOKE
HEARTS, DRAINED

BASIL LEAVES, TO GARNISH

2 Cut the peppers in half, seed and slice into strips. Set the grill to high and grill the peppers for 5-7 minutes, until charred and soft. Arrange either side of the carrots. Place the tomato wedges around the outside of the plate, sprinkle over the basil, season with salt and pepper and pour over 2 tbls of the olive oil.

3 Thinly slice the mushrooms and place in a bowl. Pour the remaining 2 tbls olive oil and 1 tbls lemon juice over the top. Add the remaining garlic and all the capers. Season to taste with salt and pepper. Mix well and then arrange on the platter. Place the olives and artichokes on the platter and garnish with basil leaves.

1 Blanch the grated carrots in boiling water for 45 seconds, drain and place in a mixing bowl. Pour 2 tbls olive oil and 1 tbls lemon juice over the top, then sprinkle over the finely chopped parsley and half the crushed garlic. Season with salt and pepper to taste. Mix together then arrange down the centre of a large oval platter.

SERVE THIS MEDITERRANEAN-STYLE HORS D'OEUVRE PLAT-TER WITH TOASTED BREAD RUBBED WITH FRESH GARLIC CLOVES AND LIGHTLY SPRINK-LED WITH OLIVE OIL.

BAKED EGGS WITH SPINACH

Ian O'Leary

When you want a dish for a lazy Sunday brunch this nutritious recipe fits the bill. Serve it with hot buttered toast.

PREPARATION TIME: 10 MINS
COOKING TIME: 10 MINS
SERVES 4

I N G R E D I E N T S

2 TBLS OIL

1 ONION, PEELED AND FINELY SLICED

225 G/8 OZ FRESH SPINACH, SHREDDED

100 G/4 OZ SMOKED HAM, CUT INTO STRIPS

4 LARGE TOMATOES, PEELED, SEEDED AND CHOPPED

4 EGGS

SALT AND GROUND BLACK PEPPER

PINCH OF THYME

4 ANCHOVIES, CUT IN HALF LENGTHWAYS, TO GARNISH

2 Divide the spinach mixture between 4 small ovenproof dishes. Arrange circles of chopped tomato around the edges. Crack an egg into the centre of each dish.

3 Season the eggs with salt and pepper and sprinkle with thyme. Put 2 strips of anchovy in a cross over each egg. Cover with foil. Stand the 4 dishes on a baking tray and bake for 5-10 minutes. Serve immediately.

m COOK 2 DISHES AT A TIME IN THE MICROWAVE. PIERCE EACH EGG YOLK WITH A COCK-TAIL STICK AND COVER WITH PIERCED CLING FILM. MICRO-WAVE ON HIGH (100%) FOR 2-3½ MINUTES OR UNTIL THE EGGS HAVE COOKED. LEAVE TO STAND FOR 2 MINUTES.

1 Preheat the oven to 200 C/400 F/ Gas 6. Heat the oil in a frying-pan, add the onion and cook for 5 minutes or until softened. Add the shredded spinach and strips of ham to the pan, cover and cook until the spinach has wilted. Remove from the heat.

TIP

FOR A VEGETARIAN VERSION, REPLACE THE HAM WITH GRATED CHEDDAR CHEESE AND ADD GROUND NUTMEG INSTEAD OF THYME. GARNISH WITH RED PEPPER.

PRAWN VOL-AU-VENTS

Ian O'Leary

These professional and tasty vol-au-vents may be fiddly to make, but are a good start to a meal for fish lovers.

PREPARATION TIME: 20 MINS
+ CHILLING
COOKING TIME: 40 MINS
SERVES 4

I N G R E D I E N T S

200 G/7 OZ PUFF PASTRY,
THAWED IF FROZEN

1 EGG, BEATEN

4 WHOLE PRAWNS, TO GARNISH

PARSLEY, TO GARNISH

FOR THE FILLING

25 G/1 OZ BUTTER

1 SMALL LEEK, ROUGHLY CHOPPED

2 TBLS FLOUR

225 ML/8 FL OZ MILK

SALT AND GROUND BLACK PEPPER

175 G/6 OZ PEELED PRAWNS

75 G/3 OZ BUTTON MUSHROOMS,
QUARTERED

1 TBLS FINELY CHOPPED PARSLEY

2 For the filling, melt the butter in a pan, add the leek and cook for 5 minutes. Stir in the flour, remove from heat and stir in the milk. Season. Cook for 3-4 minutes, stirring constantly. Stir in the prawns, mushrooms and parsley and cook for 3-4 minutes.

3 Preheat the oven to 200 C/400 F/ Gas 6. Brush the vol-au-vents with beaten egg and bake in the centre of the oven for 20-25 minutes until well risen and dry.

1 Roll out the pastry onto a lightly floured surface to 3 mm/⅛ in thick. Then cut out eight 7.5 cm/ 3 in diamond shapes with a knife or pastry cutter. Cut out four centres, leaving a 12 mm/½ in border. Score the four pastry tops with a sharp knife. Brush around the tops of the remaining pastry bases with beaten egg. Place the pastry tops on the bases and transfer to a roasting tin or baking tray. Rest the vol-au-vent cases in the fridge for 1 hour before cooking.

4 Remove the centres of the vol-au-vents with a sharp knife, spoon in the prawn filling and return to the oven for a few minutes to warm. Garnish with whole prawns and flat-leaved parsley sprigs and serve immediately.

COMPLEMENT THE FLAVOUR OF THESE DELECTABLE VOL-AU-VENTS WITH A BOTTLE OF WELL-CHILLED CHABLIS OR OTHER DRY WHITE WINE.

SCAMPI IN SHELLS

Alan Newnham

Scrumptious scampi are served in scallop
shells, which are piped with mashed potato to
create interesting little shellfish 'boats'.

PREPARATION TIME: 15 MINS
COOKING TIME: 25 MINS
SERVES 4

I N G R E D I E N T S

SALT AND GROUND BLACK PEPPER
450 G/1 LB POTATOES, PEELED
3 TBLS MILK
100 G/4 OZ BUTTON MUSHROOMS
25 G/1 OZ BUTTER
225 G/8 OZ SCAMPI, PEELED
1 CLOVE OF GARLIC, CRUSHED
4 TBLS DRY WHITE WINE
150 ML/¼ PT SINGLE CREAM
CORIANDER, TO GARNISH
LEMON SLICES, TO GARNISH

2 Thinly slice the mushrooms. Melt the butter in a frying-pan, add the mushrooms, scampi and garlic and cook for 2 minutes then remove from pan. Add the wine and cream and bring to the boil. Boil rapidly for 5 minutes or until the sauce is reduced by two-thirds. Season to taste with salt and pepper and return the scampi, mushrooms and garlic to the pan to heat through in the sauce.

1 Scald four scallop shells in boiling water then pat dry. Cut the potatoes into even-sized pieces and cook in boiling salted water for 10 minutes or until tender. Drain and mash together with the milk, salt and pepper. Using a star-shaped nozzle pipe the potato around the edges of the scallop shells. Keep warm.

3 Preheat the grill. Remove the scampi mixture from the heat and spoon into scallop shells. Place the shells under the grill and cook for 5 minutes or until golden. Serve immediately garnished with sprigs of coriander and twists of lemon.

 SCAMPI IN SCALLOP SHELLS CAN BE MADE IN ADVANCE AND KEPT IN THE FREEZER FOR UP TO 3 MONTHS, BUT MAKE SURE THEY ARE DEFROSTED THOROUGHLY BEFORE BEING REHEATED AND SERVED.

SEAFOOD MORSELS

Prepare the fish and squid in advance. Fry
each portion separately and serve in minutes
with oyster sauce-flavoured mayonnaise.

Michael Michaels

PREPARATION TIME: 1 HOUR
COOKING TIME: 10 MINS
SERVES 4

I N G R E D I E N T S

350 G/12 OZ WHITE FISH FILLETS

225 G/8 OZ BABY SQUID

SALT AND GROUND BLACK PEPPER

100 G/4 OZ WHITEBAIT

100 G/4 OZ SMALL SPRATS

100 G/4 OZ PEELED PRAWNS

100 G/4 OZ FLOUR

1 TBLS CORNFLOUR

1 EGG, SEPARATED

225 ML/8 FL OZ MILK

150 ML/¼ PT MAYONNAISE

1 TBLS OYSTER SAUCE

OIL, FOR DEEP-FRYING

1 LEMON, SLICED

SPRIGS OF PARSLEY, TO GARNISH

minutes. Whisk the egg white until stiff and then fold into the batter.

3 Spoon the mayonnaise into a bowl and stir in the oyster sauce. Heat the oil for deep-frying in a pan. Divide the fish between 4 plates – it's easiest to cook one serving at a time.

4 Dip the fish and squid in the batter, starting with the sprats. Cook in the oil until the batter is golden brown. Remove and shake off excess oil. Drain on kitchen paper. Serve each helping garnished with a slice or two of lemon and a sprig of parsley.

TIP

IF YOU LIKE HOT FLAVOURS, SOAK A PINCH OF WASABI POWDER (JAPANESE HORSE-RADISH) IN 2 TSP COLD WATER FOR 10 MINUTES — IT NEEDS THIS TIME TO BRING OUT THE FLAVOUR. ADD AS MUCH AS YOU DARE TO THE SAUCE — IT'S HOT STUFF!

1 Cut the fish fillets into 7.5 x 12 mm/3 x ½ in goujons. Pull the head and tentacles from the squid. Cut off the fins. Rub off the purplish skin using salt to help. Remove any innards and the quill-like bone. Cut into circles. Rinse all the fish well. Drain.

2 Make a batter by sifting the flour, cornflour and salt into a bowl. Make a well in the centre and beat in the egg yolk and milk. Leave for 10

ARTICHOKE POTS

Clint Brown

Make a hearty start to the meal with these
little pots of artichoke hearts baked with
Parmesan cheese and bacon.

PREPARATION TIME: 10 MINS
COOKING TIME: 20 MINS
SERVES 4

INGREDIENTS

2 TBLS BUTTER
2 SHALLOTS, FINELY CHOPPED
3 SLICES STREAKY BACON, CHOPPED
400 G/14 OZ TINNED ARTICHOKE HEARTS, DRAINED AND CHOPPED
125 ML/4 FL OZ DOUBLE CREAM
50 G/2 OZ PARMESAN CHEESE, GRATED
1 EGG YOLK
½ TSP FINELY CHOPPED FRESH TARRAGON
SALT AND GROUND BLACK PEPPER

1 Preheat the oven to 200 C/400 F/ Gas 6. Melt half the butter in a saucepan, add the shallots and cook over a gentle heat for 3 minutes or until softened.

2 Transfer to a bowl, add the bacon, artichoke hearts, cream, half the cheese, egg yolk and the chopped tarragon. Season with salt and ground black pepper.

3 Spoon the mixture into 4 ramekins, sprinkle the remaining Parmesan cheese over the top and dot with the rest of the butter.

4 Put the ramekins on a baking tray and bake in the centre of the oven for 15 minutes. Serve.

 THESE ARTICHOKE POTS CAN BE SERVED AS A STARTER TO A LIGHT FISH MAIN COURSE OR WITH A MIXED SALAD AND WARM CRUSTY ROLLS.

m COVER THE RAMEKINS WITH MICROWAVE-PROOF CLING FILM AND COOK ON MEDIUM HIGH (75%) FOR 4 MINUTES. PLACE UNDER A HOT GRILL UNTIL GOLDEN BROWN.

TIP

FOR VEGETARIANS REPLACE THE BACON WITH 25 G/1 OZ CHOPPED WALNUTS.

SURF & TURF KEBABS

Clint Brown

Succulent bite-sized pieces of beef with fresh prawns dipped into Blue Cheese or Thousand Island dressing. Serve as a starter or appetiser.

42

PREPARATION TIME: 10 MINS
COOKING TIME: 6-8 MINS
SERVES 4

I N G R E D I E N T S

225 G/8 OZ FILLET OF BEEF

16 LARGE PRAWNS, PEELED

2 TBLS SESAME OIL

CHOPPED PARSLEY, TO GARNISH

LEMON WEDGES, TO SERVE

FOR THE BLUE CHEESE DRESSING

100 G/4 OZ BLUE CHEESE

150 ML/¼ PT SOURED CREAM

2-3 DROPS TABASCO

FOR THOUSAND ISLAND DIP

5 TBLS SALAD CREAM

1 TBLS TOMATO PUREE

1 TBLS LEMON JUICE

2-3 DROPS WORCESTERSHIRE SAUCE

2 To make the dips: crumble the blue cheese into a bowl, stir in the soured cream and add the Tabasco. Mix together the salad cream, tomato purée, lemon juice and Worcestershire sauce. Pour into separate serving dishes and chill.

1 Cut beef into 24 cubes. Thread meat and prawns alternately onto 8 small kebab sticks so that each kebab contains 3 cubes of meat and 2 prawns. Put kebabs on a grill rack and brush with the sesame oil.

3 Grill kebabs under a high heat for 6-8 minutes, brushing with sesame oil and turning occasionally. Garnish the dips with chopped parsley and serve with the kebabs and lemon wedges.

 ALTERNATIVELY, COOK THE KEBABS ON A BARBECUE OR SERVE AS AN ACCOMPANIMENT TO A FONDUE.

TIP

THIS STARTER CAN BE PREPARED SEVERAL HOURS OR EVEN THE DAY BEFORE A MEAL, AS MARINATING IN SESAME OIL ENHANCES THE FLAVOUR OF BOTH THE MEAT AND PRAWNS.

MOZZARELLA & TOMATO PARCELS

Clint Brown

Tomatoes, basil and melting mozzarella cheese are wrapped in crisp filo pastry to make delicious parcels with a Mediterranean flavour. Serve as a party snack or starter.

PREPARATION TIME: 30 MINS
COOKING TIME: 10-15 MINS
MAKES 25

INGREDIENTS

450 G/1 LB SMALL TOMATOES, CHOPPED

BUNCH OF SPRING ONIONS, TRIMMED AND FINELY SLICED

3 TBLS FINELY CHOPPED FRESH BASIL

SALT AND GROUND BLACK PEPPER

10 SHEETS FILO PASTRY, THAWED

100 G/4 OZ MELTED BUTTER, PLUS EXTRA FOR GREASING

275 G/10 OZ MOZZARELLA CHEESE, FINELY CHOPPED

25 G/1 OZ SESAME SEEDS

BASIL, CURLY ENDIVE AND BATAVIA, TO GARNISH

1 Heat the oven to 180 C/350 F/Gas 4. Mix the tomatoes, spring onions and basil in a bowl and season with salt and pepper.

2 Lay 1 sheet of filo pastry on a chopping board. Brush with melted butter and lay a second sheet on top. Cut the rectangle widthways into 5 even strips.

TIP

MOZZARELLA CAN ALSO BE BOUGHT IN 225 G/8 OZ VACUUM PACKS OR IN SMALL BALLS STORED IN LIQUID.

3 Place 1 tbls of the tomato mixture and 1 tbls mozzarella about 2.5 cm/1 in from the narrow bottom edge and slightly to the right. Fold the bottom left-hand corner over the filling to make a triangle and fold up in triangles until you have a neat parcel.

4 Make 25 parcels, brush with a little butter and then sprinkle with the sesame seeds. Grease 2 baking trays, place the parcels on them and cook, in batches for 10-15 minutes or until golden. Serve garnished with the basil, curly endive and batavia.

FROZEN FILO PASTRY, SOMETIMES CALLED STRUDEL PASTRY, IS SOLD IN MOST LARGE SUPERMARKETS. THAW THOROUGHLY, UNWRAP AND REMOVE THE REQUIRED NUMBER OF SHEETS AND KEEP THEM MOIST UNDER A DAMP CLOTH. REFREEZE ANY REMAINING SHEETS OF PASTRY.

STUFFED TOMATOES

Alan Newnham

These stuffed tomatoes taste equally good
served hot or cold. Garnish with basil leaves
before serving.

PREPARATION TIME: 20 MINS
COOKING TIME: 10 MINS
SERVES 4

INGREDIENTS

50 G/2 OZ CRACKED WHEAT

4 BEEFSTEAK TOMATOES

BUNCH SPRING ONIONS, TRIMMED
AND FINELY CHOPPED

1 COURGETTE, VERY FINELY
CHOPPED

3 CLOVES OF GARLIC, CRUSHED

2 TBLS FINELY CHOPPED PARSLEY

2 TBLS FINELY CHOPPED MINT

1 TBLS OLIVE OIL

SALT AND GROUND BLACK PEPPER

3 Chop the drained tomato pulp into small pieces and add the spring onions, courgette, garlic, parsley, mint and oil and mix well. Drain the cracked wheat and add to the other ingredients. Season with salt and pepper and spoon the mixture back into the tomato shells while still warm.

1 Preheat the oven to 180 C/350 F/ Gas 4. Put the cracked wheat into a heat-proof bowl and pour over enough boiling water to cover. Leave to soak for 10 minutes.

4 Score the tomato shells and tops with a small sharp knife and place on a baking tray. Cook for 10 minutes until the tomatoes are heated through and the stuffing is hot. Serve.

2 Meanwhile cut the tops off the tomatoes and scoop out the tomato pulp with a spoon, leaving a sturdy shell to stuff. Place half of the pulp in a sieve to drain over a bowl and set the remainder aside.

TIP

DON'T WASTE THE RESERVED TOMATO PULP. USE IT TO GIVE EXTRA FLAVOUR TO TOMATO SAUCE.

ARTICHOKES & TARRAGON BUTTER

Ian O'Leary

Globe artichokes are delicious when you pull the leaves off and dip them in this herby butter. Preparing the artichokes too, is easy just follow the step-by-step instructions.

PREPARATION TIME: 10 MINS
COOKING TIME: 30-40 MINS
SERVES 2

I N G R E D I E N T S

2 LARGE GLOBE ARTICHOKES

6 LEMON SLICES

SALT

TARRAGON SPRIGS, TO GARNISH

FOR THE TARRAGON BUTTER

75 G/3 OZ BUTTER

1 CLOVE OF GARLIC, CRUSHED

1 TBLS CHOPPED FRESH TARRAGON

3 Tie 2 lemon slices firmly to the bottom of each of the artichokes with string (this prevents the artichokes from discolouring).

4 Place in a large saucepan of salted water, bring to the boil, cover and cook for 30-40 minutes or until a leaf comes away easily if pulled. Remove the lemon and drain the artichoke upside down for 1 minute. Place on a serving dish and garnish with remaining lemon slices and tarragon sprigs.

5 Meanwhile make the tarragon butter: melt the butter over a low heat. Add the garlic and cook for 30 seconds. Pour into a serving bowl and stir in the chopped fresh tarragon. Serve with the artichokes.

1 Hold the artichokes firmly and cut off the stalks together with the first 12 mm/½ in from the bottom of the artichoke.

 SERVE EACH PERSON WITH THEIR OWN POT OF TARRAGON BUTTER TO DIP THE LEAVES IN, AND A SIDE PLATE FOR THE DEBRIS. OR TRY SERVING THE ARTICHOKES COLD WITH A FRENCH DRESSING, OR MAYONNAISE WITH A STIFFLY BEATEN EGG WHITE ADDED.

2 Turn the artichokes round, hold firmly and slice off the top 12 mm/½ in of the leaves. Snip away the points from the lower leaves.

DEVILLED MUSHROOM CUPS

Clint Brown

Quick and easy to make, Devilled Mushroom Cups can be served as a starter or a party snack. Make them in advance then reheat them just before serving.

PREPARATION TIME: 15 MINS
COOKING TIME: 30 MINS
SERVES 4

I N G R E D I E N T S

4 LARGE THIN SLICES OF WHITE
BREAD

75 G/3 OZ MELTED BUTTER

50 G/2 OZ PICKLING ONIONS

1 THICK GAMMON STEAK, CUT INTO
SHORT STICKS

225 G/8 OZ MUSHROOMS, CHOPPED

1 TBLS WORCESTERSHIRE SAUCE

1 TSP TOMATO PUREE

SALT AND GROUND BLACK PEPPER

2 TBLS SOURED CREAM

4 SPRIGS OF CHERVIL, TO GARNISH

3 Meanwhile make the filling: fry the onions and gammon in the remaining 25 g/1 oz butter until lightly browned. Add the mushrooms and fry quickly at first to brown the mushrooms, then turn the heat down and cook slowly until all the mushroom juice has evaporated. Gently stir in the Worcestershire sauce, tomato purée and salt and pepper to taste.

1 Preheat the oven to 200 C/400 F/ Gas 6. Use a large biscuit cutter to stamp the bread into rounds. Soak the rounds in 50 g/2 oz of the melted butter and use to line 4 tartlet moulds. Put an empty tartlet tray on top to hold the bread in shape as it cooks. If you don't have a second tartlet tray, cover the buttered bread cases with greaseproof paper and fill with rice to hold them down.

2 Bake for 10 minutes then remove the top tray or greaseproof paper and rice. Bake for a further 10 minutes to allow the bottoms to brown and become crispy.

Diana Miller

4 Fill the toast shells with the filling mixture then spoon the soured cream over the top. Garnish with the chervil sprigs and serve.

TIP

DEVILLED MUSHROOM CUPS CAN BE MADE IN ADVANCE: REHEAT THE TOAST SHELLS AND FILLING SEPARATELY, THEN ASSEMBLE JUST BEFORE SERVING.

GARLIC MUSHROOMS

A simple and delicious starter – tiny button mushrooms fried with a little bacon and more than just a hint of garlic. Serve them with warm crispy French bread.

PREPARATION TIME: 5 MINS
COOKING TIME: 15 MINS
SERVES 4

I N G R E D I E N T S

450 G/1 LB SMALL BUTTON
MUSHROOMS

40 G/1 ½ OZ BUTTER

2 RASHERS STREAKY BACON, VERY
THINLY SLICED

3 CLOVES OF GARLIC, CRUSHED

25 G/1 OZ BREADCRUMBS

2 TBLS PARSLEY, FINELY CHOPPED

SALT AND GROUND BLACK PEPPER

1 TBLS LEMON JUICE

LEMON SLICES, TO GARNISH

PARSLEY, TO GARNISH

2 Mix together the bacon, garlic, breadcrumbs, parsley and seasoning and sprinkle over the mushrooms. Cook, uncovered, over a very gentle heat for 10 minutes, stirring the ingredients frequently.

3 Add the lemon juice and adjust the seasoning. Serve immediately, garnished with the lemon slices and the parsley.

m MELT THE BUTTER IN A LARGE MICROWAVE-PROOF BOWL FOR 1 MINUTE ON HIGH (100%). ADD IN THE MUSHROOMS AND COOK UNCOVERED FOR 3 MIN-UTES. STIR IN THE REST OF THE INGREDIENTS, BLEND TOGETHER WELL, AND THEN COOK IN THE MICROWAVE FOR A FURTHER 5 MINUTES.

1 Wipe the mushrooms and cut in half if large. Melt the butter in a pan and fry the mushrooms for 3 minutes until brown.

TIP

THERE'S NO NEED TO RESTRICT YOUR-SELF TO BUTTON MUSHROOMS IF YOU LIKE TO EXPERIMENT WITH DIFFERENT KINDS OF FUNGI — CEPS, SHIITAKE AND OYSTER MUSHROOMS CAN ALL BE COOKED IN THIS WAY AND LEND THEIR OWN INDIVIDUAL TASTE TO THE DISH.

SWISS GRUYERE CREPES

Clint Brown

Try these cheesy crêpes, served with a tangy
salad, as a substantial starter or as a delicious
light meal on their own.

PREPARATION TIME: 15 MINS
+ CHILLING
COOKING TIME: 10 MINS
SERVES 4

INGREDIENTS

8 x 15 CM/6 IN CREPES OR PAN-
CAKES, AVAILABLE PRE-PREPARED
FROM MAJOR SUPERMARKETS

175 G/6 OZ GRUYERE CHEESE,
GRATED

1 LARGE EGG, BEATEN

225 G/8 OZ FINE DRIED WHITE
BREADCRUMBS

OIL, FOR DEEP-FRYING

TO SERVE

2 HEADS OF CHICORY

2 PEELED ORANGES, DIVIDED INTO
SEGMENTS

12 WALNUTS, SHELLED

FOR THE GARNISH

THIN SLICES OF LEMON

SPRIGS OF WATERCRESS

2 Coat the crêpe triangles first in the beaten egg, then in the breadcrumbs. Leave in the fridge for 30 minutes to help prevent the triangles opening up when fried.

3 Heat the oil in a large heavy-based saucepan or deep-fat fryer to 190 C/375 F, then fry the crêpes in two batches, until golden and crisp. Place on a dish, lined with kitchen paper, and keep warm in a very low oven.

4 Meanwhile, split up the heads of chicory and use 8 leaves to form a flower pattern on each plate. Place segments of orange and halved walnuts on alternate leaves and one walnut in the centre. Garnish the crêpes with slices of lemon and sprigs of watercress and serve with the chicory salad.

1 Sprinkle each crêpe, on one side, with grated cheese. Then, fold each crêpe in half and half again, so it forms a triangle.

 BLEND TOGETHER MAYON-
NAISE, WATERCRESS, LEMON
JUICE AND SEASONING AND
SERVE WITH THE CREPES.

CHEESE & HERB OMELETTE

Clint Brown

This light and tasty omelette is easy to make and highly nutritious. Try it with all kinds of different fillings too.

PREPARATION TIME: 10 MINS
COOKING TIME: 5 MINS
SERVES 1

I N G R E D I E N T S

2 EGGS, SEPARATED

2 TBLS FRESH CHOPPED HERBS

15 G/½ OZ BUTTER

25 G/1 OZ RED LEICESTER CHEESE,
GRATED

½ TSP GRATED PARMESAN CHEESE

1 Beat the egg yolks in a large bowl until creamy. Whisk the egg whites until stiff, then fold in the chopped herbs. Carefully fold in the egg yolks.

3 When cooked, tip the omelette out of the pan and fold over. Serve immediately, sprinkled with Parmesan cheese.

SERVE A TANGY TOMATO AND AUBERGINE RATATOUILLE WITH THE OMELETTE TO MAKE AN EVEN HEARTIER MEAL.

2 Melt the butter in a frying-pan and pour in the egg mixture. Sprinkle the cheese on the top and cook gently until the omelette base is set and a golden colour underneath.

TIP

FOR A HOT OR COLD SNACK MAKE TWO OR THREE THIN OMELETTE BASES AND ADD DIFFERENT FILLINGS. ASPARAGUS TIPS, PAN-FRIED GARLIC MUSHROOMS OR A HOME-MADE TOMATO SAUCE WOULD BE IDEAL. ALTERNATIVELY, USE GRATED SEMI-HARD CHEESE SUCH AS GRUYERE, JARLSBERG OR EDAM.

SPAGHETTI EN PAPILLOTE

Michael Michaels

Baking allows the spaghetti to soak up the full flavour of the spicy olive and tomato sauce and packs these pasta parcels with flavour.

PREPARATION TIME: 10 MINS
COOKING TIME: 25-30 MINS
SERVES 4

I N G R E D I E N T S

1 CLOVE OF GARLIC, CRUSHED

2 TBLS OLIVE OIL, PLUS EXTRA FOR
GREASING

175 G/6 OZ PASSATA

SALT AND GROUND BLACK PEPPER

450 G/1 LB TOMATOES

1 RED CHILLI

450 G/1 LB SPAGHETTI

20 BLACK OLIVES

SHREDDED BASIL, TO GARNISH

bowl of cold water, then peel, quarter and seed them. Chop the red chilli and stir into the passata mixture.

3 Put the spaghetti in a saucepan of salted boiling water and cook for 5-10 minutes, until half cooked.

1 Preheat the oven to 190 C/375 F/ Gas 5. Sauté the garlic in the olive oil. Then add the passata and mix well. Season and cook over a medium heat for 2-3 minutes.

2 Put the whole tomatoes in a saucepan of boiling water and simmer for 1 minute. Transfer to a

4 Brush parchment paper with oil and cut into 4 pieces. Mix the pasta with the passata, olives and tomatoes. Season with salt and pepper. Divide equally between the pieces of parchment paper. Wrap the paper tightly, twisting each end. Bake for 15 minutes. When cooked, slit parcels with a knife and sprinkle fresh basil over each serving.

TIP

PASSATA IS PUREED, SIEVED TOMATOES WHICH CAN BE BOUGHT FROM LARGE SUPERMARKETS IN BOTTLES AND CAR-TONS. TO MAKE YOUR OWN, SIMPLY PUREE AND SIEVE TINNED TOMATOES.

PARMA HAM STUFFED PASTA

Simon Wheeler

Parma ham, bought in large thin slices, gives this dish its distinctive flavour. It may seem a bit costly but don't worry – you won't need much as a little goes a long way.

PREPARATION TIME: 20 MINS
COOKING TIME: 20 MINS
SERVES 4

INGREDIENTS

3 BEEFSTEAK TOMATOES
2 TBLS OLIVE OIL
SALT
1 SPRIG OF ROSEMARY
16 BASIL LEAVES
225 ML/8 FL OZ SINGLE CREAM
2 EGG YOLKS
50 G/2 OZ FRESH PARMESAN CHEESE, GRATED
1 TBLS TOMATO PUREE
20 LARGE PASTA SHELLS
40 G/1 ½ OZ BUTTER
225 G/8 OZ BUTTON MUSHROOMS
100 G/4 OZ PARMA HAM, CUT INTO STRIPS

3 Place the pasta shells in a large pan of salted boiling water: cook for 10 minutes until tender. Chop the reserved tomato flesh and shred the remaining basil. Heat the butter until frothy. Add the mushrooms and cook over a high heat for 2 minutes until golden. Add the parma ham and heat through, stirring to separate the strips.

4 Add the chopped tomato and shredded basil leaves at the last moment. Drain the pasta and spoon the stuffing into the shells. Place a quarter of the sieved tomato sauce on each of 4 plates. Arrange 5 stuffed shells on top of each and serve.

1 Skin tomatoes cut into quarters. Remove the seeds and core and chop them roughly. Reserve outer flesh. Gently cook core, oil and salt for 5 minutes until pulped. Add the rosemary and 6 of the basil leaves and cook for another 1-2 minutes. Sieve.

2 Beat together the cream, egg yolks and parmesan cheese. Pour into frying-pan and heat very gently, stirring constantly, until the mixture thickens but does not boil. Stir in the tomato liquid and tomato purée. Set aside and keep warm.

TIP

TRY TO USE FRESH PARMESAN CHEESE FOR THIS DISH. THE READY-GRATED VARIETY DOESN'T MELT AS WELL AND GIVES THE SAUCE A GRAINY TEXTURE. IF YOU HAVE TO USE READY-GRATED PARMESAN, HOWEVER, STRAIN THE SAUCE THROUGH A FINE SIEVE BEFORE ADDING THE TOMATO LIQUID AND TOMATO PUREE. GARNISH THE FINISHED DISH WITH BASIL SPRIGS BEFORE SERVING.

TAGLIATELLE WITH SMOKED SALMON

Paul Moon

Flavours and colours combine elegantly in this starter. Tagliatelle is moulded into a tower, and luxuriously garnished with strips of smoked salmon.

PREPARATION TIME: 5 MINS
COOKING TIME: 10 MINS
SERVES 4

INGREDIENTS

225 G/8 OZ FRESH TAGLIATELLE, RED, GREEN AND WHITE
BUTTER, FOR GREASING
100 G/4 OZ SMOKED SALMON, CUT INTO STRIPS
4 SMALL TOMATOES, SKINNED, SEEDED AND FINELY CHOPPED
2 TSP LUMPFISH ROE
FRESH DILL FRONDS, TO GARNISH
FOR THE SAUCE
225 ML/8 FL OZ DOUBLE CREAM
1 EGG YOLK
1 TBLS FINELY CHOPPED DILL
50 G/2 OZ GORGONZOLA CHEESE
SALT AND GROUND BLACK PEPPER

3 Divide the pasta between 4 greased dariole moulds. Using the back of a spoon press a layer of red, green and white tagliatelle into the moulds, finishing with a red layer. Place a serving plate on top of each mould, turn over and invert onto the plates. Remove the moulds carefully.

1 Cook the pasta in a pan of boiling water for 3-4 minutes until softened but still firm. Drain and rinse under hot running water.

2 Make the sauce: put the cream, egg yolk, finely chopped dill, Gorgonzola cheese and salt and pepper into a small saucepan and place over a gentle heat. Cook, stirring constantly for 5 minutes, until the sauce is slightly thickened.

Clint Brown

4 Arrange the strips of salmon and finely chopped tomato in little mounds around the edges of the plates. Top with roe and place fronds of dill in alternate spaces between the tomatoes and salmon. Pour the sauce over the pasta and serve immediately.

TIP

AS AN ALTERNATIVE, YOU CAN USE GRAVADLAX INSTEAD OF SALMON AND SOURED CREAM INSTEAD OF CREAM.

IF YOU'D LIKE TO SERVE WINE WITH THIS STARTER, CHOOSE A GLASS OF WELL-CHILLED ROSE DE LOIRE.

INDEX